A SONG OF JOY AND OTHER POEMS

A Song of Joy and Other Poems has all of the splendid qualities of Byron Herbert Reece's two earlier volumes of poetry plus a deepening awareness of death.

Byron Herbert Reece's poetry stems directly from his own region in Georgia and its richness of balladry, and from the immense resources of Biblical lore. All of this heritage, great as it is, would mean little, however, were it not for his own spirit and special quality, seen in his prose as well as in his poetry, which has an unerring rightness and magnificence.

A Song of Joy and Other Poems is divided into three sections: (I) A Song of Joy; (II) A Song of Dura and Others; (III) Songs for Breath. Mr. Reece has concluded this present volume in an interesting, unusual and very touching manner, with three Epigraphs referring to his three previously published works: *Bow Down in Jericho, Better a Dinner of Herbs*, and *Ballad of the Bones*.

Mr. Reece's poetry reflects a tragic sense of life but also a great resonant joy and belief in its ultimate glory—a largeness which originates in his favorite source book, the Bible.

BYRON HERBERT REECE
(1917-1958)

Byron Herbert Reece was born and reared in a secluded mountain area of North Georgia near Blairsville. Before he entered elementary school, he read *Pilgrim's Progress* and much of the Bible, upon which many of his later ballads were based. As an adult, he was a lonely mountain man who was a modestly successful dirt farmer and a poet of surpassing genius. Reece had the ability to say new things in the old traditional forms, distinguished by their simplicity and accuracy. His poetry was mystical, lonely and often seemed preoccupied with death. Reece was perhaps the greatest balladeer of the Applachians. During his short life, he received two prestigious Guggenheim awards and lectured as Writer-in-Residence at UCLA, Emory University and Young Harris College. Reece died by his own hand on the campus of Young Harris College in early June 1958.

Other Cherokee titles by Byron Herbert Reece:

>*Ballad of the Bones & Other Poems*
>*Better a Dinner of Herbs*
>*Bow Down in Jericho*
>*The Hawk and the Sun*
>*The Season of Flesh*

also: *Mountain Singer: The Life and the Legacy of Byron Herbert Reece* by Raymond A. Cook

A SONG OF JOY

And Other Poems

By BYRON HERBERT REECE

Poetry

THE BALLAD OF THE BONES

BOW DOWN IN JERICHO

A SONG OF JOY AND OTHER POEMS

Fiction

BETTER A DINNER OF HERBS

A SONG OF JOY

And Other Poems

By

BYRON HERBERT REECE

Cherokee Publishing Company
Atlanta, Georgia
1985

Library of Congress Cataloging-in-Publication Data

Reece, Byron Herbert, 1917-1958.
    A song of joy, and other poems.

    I. Title.
PS3535.E245S6   1985   811'.54   85-22355
ISBN 0-87797-105-6 (alk. paper)

Copyright © 1952, by E. P. Dutton & Co., Inc.

This book is printed on acid-free paper which conforms to the American National Standard Z39.48-1984 *Permanence of Paper for Printed Library Materials.* Paper that conforms to this standard's requirements for pH, alkaline reserve and freedom from groundwood is anticipated to last several hundred years without significant deterioration under normal library use and storage conditions. ∞

Manufactured in the United States of America

ISBN: 0-87797-309-1

Published by arrangement with
E. P. Dutton, a division of New American Library

CHEROKEE PUBLISHING COMPANY
P.O. Box 1730, Marietta, GA 30061

TABLE OF CONTENTS

I

A SONG OF JOY

II

A SONG OF DURA

And Others

III

SONGS FOR BREATH

[5]

CONTENTS

[6]

CONTENTS

THREE EPIGRAPHS

I

A SONG OF JOY

A SONG OF JOY

Saying, How better
  Could I employ
The tithe of my time
  Than in searching for joy?

I arose in the morning
  And took to the road,
And the strength of my yearning
  Was a guide and a goad.

Eschewing plunder,
  Avoiding strife,
I rode forth under
  The leaves of life.

I came on sorrow
  Before the sun
Had climbed the ladder
  Of hours to one.

Must I see sorrow,
  I said, her face
Today, tomorrow
  In every place

While joy is hiding?
  I found joy not
Though I went riding
  By many a spot

Where joy had bidden,
    As I was told,
Though cloaked and hidden,
    In days of old.

I rode by the priest
    Was saying his Matin,
I rode by the scholar
    Was reading his Latin.

The priest was grouchy,
    The hour was too early;
The Latin was hard
    And the scholar was surly.

I rode by the miller
    Was grinding the grain;
I rode by the farmer
    Was plowing the plain.

The miller had sorrow
    To be his bread;
From sorrow's acre
    Was the farmer fed.

I rode the seasons
    By fours around
And came on reasons:
    No joy I found.

So I cried to the sage
    As I passed him by:
What or where
    Is joy? cried I.

My horse's feet
  On the pavement rang
But through their beat
  The sooth sage sang:

Joy is a hind
  That knows no tether,
Joy is a bird
  On a flying feather.

Should either falter
  So you might find him
So would he alter
  And you not mind him.

       ❖   ❖   ❖

I rode forth under
  The temporal leaf
And mid the morning
  I came on grief.

The mother was crying
  Above her son
Wounded and dying;
  And I rode on.

The lover was weeping
  Her blighted troth
Too cleft for keeping;
  I left her loath.

A black man wept
    His cast of color;
I rode forth bearing
    His cry of dolor.

The pleas of the hungry children
    Rent
The hearts of their fathers;
    And on I went.

I cried to the parson
    As I passed him by:
O what or where
    Is joy? cried I.

My horse's feet
    On the pavement rang
But through their beat
    The parson sang:

Joy is foreign
    To man's estate;
Joy in heaven
    The saints await.

Should joy dissemble
    In its abode
False were the gamble
    Of heaven's road.

❖   ❖   ❖

Under the roof
   Time's long leaves rear
Rang my horse's hoof,
   And I came on fear.

The rich were fearing
   Their riches' sack;
They with no money
   Were fearing its lack.

The idle were fearing
   The loss of ease;
The hale were fearing
   Fell disease.

The poor were fearing
   Their low estate;
The harmed were fearing
   The tooth of hate.

The proud were fearing
   The loss of pride;
The groom was fearing
   To take the bride

Lest she be stricken
   Somehence and lost
And his heart sicken
   To count the cost.

The strong were fearing
   Their fading strength;
The weak were fearing
   To match their length

Against the mattress
    Made of earth
In the final fortress
    Of impregnable girth.

The knight was fearing
    To take the road;
But I was faring
    Before the goad.

*   *   *

And I came to madness
    And began to sing:
O Joy, be a bird
    On a broken wing

Bright and fleeing
    With startled speech
But, wounded being,
    Within my reach.

Bide back of a door
    With a broken hasp
That I may gather you
    Into my grasp.

Or be as the risen
    And sunken sun
About a prison
    Of space to run,

Each day renewing
  Till I grow blind,
Insensate, suing
  That earth be kind

And dark Death harken
  My broken lisp
And blot and darken
  The will-of-the-wisp

Of flying joy
  That gainless led
The ageless boy
  To the aged's bed,

With shroud for sheet
  And earth for pillow
And rain to beat
  A plaint of willow.

❋   ❋   ❋

But joy heard not,
  I wasted my breath;
And I rode forth
  And came on Death.

One by one
  And mound by mound
I raised up shrines
  In graveyard ground.

But a space for prayer
   Above their sod
I scarce could spare
   From the quest I rode

Until, with time's hand
   At my throat,
By the last bier
   I paused to note

The look of peace
   My dead did wear,
And then I paused
   And made a prayer:

O Death, I cried,
   Ender of strife,
Whose lips have not lied
   Like the lips of life,

Fulfilling all
   Thou promiseth,
Or thou befall,
   Hear me, O Death,

And once before
   Your spell employ
Open one door
   And show me joy!

Death to our seeming
   Is less than air;
The lungs in breathing
   Forbid him there.

Death is less
  Than a drift of rain;
Fleet blood forbids him
  Along the vein.

Death is less
  Than a wooden splinter;
The heart in beating
  Forbids him enter.

But Death is greater
  Than sight or sound;
His bottomless crater
  The world drops down.

Death is greater
  Than reach of sight;
His dark dominion
  Encompasses light.

For Death the giant
  The universe
Is ten times round
  To wheel his hearse.

But I was humble
  And Death was kind,
And Death was willing
  To pay me mind.

"Before I slake you
  Of all desire,
Behold, I will take you,
  As you require,

"A backward journey
From man to boy
And open wide doors
And show you joy."

II

And we two turning,
Death and I
Rode under the burning
Evening sky.

Day hung at rest,
Then morning-wise
The sun in the west
Began to rise.

Pale in their pastures
Every beast
His early shadow
Cast toward the east.

Our horses strode
With the eastward sun
Along the road
I had come upon.

And soon we saw
In our backward search
Gravestones in the shadow
Of a church.

From God's lone acre
    Where they had lain
The dead I had buried
    Rose up again.

The coffins opened
    That bound them close
And out of the grave
    The dead arose.

And joy flooded
    My soul like rain
To see those shrouded
    Dead rise again.

And burly Death
    Began to chide:
"Had you no joy
    Or these had died?"

O Yes! I said,
    Then pierced with pain
I saw those dead
    Lie down again,

Each like a child
    Put back to bed
Pulling his mound
    Above his head.

O Death, desist,
    I cried with ruth,
And raise these dead
    In very truth!

"Under the sod
    That's under the sky
Two thousand years
    Does Lazarus lie

"Who rose him once
    From the tomb," Death said.
"I have opened one door—
    The dead are dead."

          ❋   ❋   ❋

And backward still
    I rode with Death.
We met full soon
    Upon the path

The fearful knight
    That blessings said
With joyful lips
    That no man bled

Beneath his stroke;
    And past the weak
Whose joy was greater
    Than they could speak

Because afar
    In a far place
In another hour
    Was Death to face.

In a moment
　　We rode among
The jubilation
　　Of the strong

Who each a psalm
　　Of joy made
Because his strength
　　Was yet to fade.

The groom sang joyful
　　Litanies
And all because
　　The bride was his,

More worth the getting
　　Than a bag of gold,
A sun unsetting
　　Against night's cold.

We met the proud
　　With careful stride
Bearing the treasure
　　Of their pride

Safe against
　　Their hearts of stone,
Fearing no loss
　　But pride's alone.

❀　　❀　　❀

Soon by the wayside
  Death and I
Heard the sound
  Of a lullaby.

The mother cuddled
  Her infant son;
With joy she swaddled
  The little one.

And a gay girl flirted
  Her skirts and sang,
Holding to see
  A golden ring

And a little locket
  Of silver, both
Her lover had given her
  With his troth.

And the black child lay
  In his mother's breast
And laughed till day
  Was wrecked in the west,

Never once sorry
  To lie against night
And suckle and worry
  A breast not white.

And a sound like linnets
  Came out of a hall
From children in it
  Feasting all

And their fathers fed them
  And teased them, pleased
To dandle their children
  With hunger appeased.

Sure and steady
  Our horses strode
And soon by the parson's
  House we rode.

I rose in my saddle
  As we passed by.
O Parson, where
  Is joy? cried I.

Our horses' feet
  On the pavement rang
But through their beat
  The parson sang:

Joy is present
  With every priest
And poet and peasant
  And bird and beast.

All things blooded,
  Of foot or wing,
With joy are flooded.
  Their fountains sing

Before their spilling
  To red a clod
The same song filling
  The heart of God.

Nor shall it falter
    This side the Verge,
Nor God's song alter
    As those two merge

In earth or heaven,
    In cave or air,
Each to each given,
    Who knows where?

        ❀   ❀   ❀

With one of such wisdom
    I would abide:
Death said, "We have somewhat
    Yet to ride."

So we rode past the farmer
    Was plowing the plain,
We rode past the miller
    Was grinding the grain.

The miller had joy
    To be his bread;
From acres of joy
    Was the farmer fed.

We rode by the scholar
    And heard him say:
Amo, amas, amat,
    Ego amo te.

And the priest's voice
  With a lark in it
Sent *Glorias* to God
  As if he meant it.

Keeping the road
  I had gone before
We came again soon
  To the sage's door.

As soon as his gray head
  I had spied,
O what or where
  Is joy? I cried.

Our horses' feet
  On the pavement rang
But through their beat
  The sooth sage sang:

Joy is the glimmer
  You think it not;
Joy is the simmer
  Of the filled pot.

Joy is the bird
  In the netted blind;
Joy, of the herd,
  Is the gentle hind

Quiet at your proffer
  Constrained to stand
That he may suffer
  The touch of your hand.

O deep as breath
　　Are joy's wells
And close as Death
　　Shall smite the cells!

　　　　*　　*　　*

Now I would have bidden
　　In his abode,
But as we had ridden
　　Still we rode.

Soon was the sooth sage
　　Left behind,
And Death looked inward
　　And read my mind,

The dark thought seething
　　Behind my brow:
"Art thou still breathing?"
　　Death whispered. "Now

"Before you suffer
　　My single kiss
Look, and tell me
　　What door is this

"Hinged forever
　　'Twixt night and earth?"
That, I answered,
　　Is the door of birth,

Entry and exit.
　　Death said, "True,"
And bent and kissed me
　　And I passed through.

II

A SONG OF DURA
And Others

A SONG OF DURA

I

Behold, the king of Babylon
Set up an image made of gold
Before his gates. The morning sun
In rains of riches from it rolled;
And when the evening sun was set
On Babylon, its jewelled eyes
Like double moons against the jet
Night, stared unblinking from the skies.
It was threescore cubits in height,
  Six cubits in breadth,
    And it stood on the Plain of Dura
    In the province of Babylon.

The king sat kingly in his hall,
And all his minions standing by
Looked on the king so royal
Then on themselves, and turned to sigh
Because they each were not a king.
But him they envied to behold
Looked always at a single thing,
Stared at the god he made of gold.

And now and then he touched his lips
Then with his fingers touched his brow,
Or rose, inclining from the hips,
And made the One a kingly bow;
But still the god that he had made
Noticed him not; aloof, immense,
It stood unmoved through shine and shade
And stared him out of countenance.

And so the king was filled with fear
The One was wroth that he alone
Looked on the gold god to revere;
Therefore were nimble runners gone
To bid his kingdom come in haste
To bow before the god and sing
His praise while on their knees debased;
Then might the god behold the King!

The nimble runners hurried forth
Through all Chadnezzar's land to call,
From east and west and south and north
To gather in his audience hall,
The princes
  The governors
    The captains
      The judges
        The treasurers
          The counselors
            The sheriffs
              And all the rulers of the provinces.

And soon the plain of Dura heard
The thunder of the hosts that trod
Each other down to heed the word
Of him that made the mighty god
Threescore cubits in height
  Six cubits in breadth
    That stood on the Plain of Dura
      In the province of Babylon.

Now when the people all were come
Into the presence of the king
The herald sounded on his drum
Three notes, and cried abroad the thing
The king commanded him to say
At dawn of Dedication Day
To the Princes
  The governors
    The captains
     The judges
      The treasurers
       The counselors
       The sheriffs
        And all the rulers of the provinces:

The king of Babylon has made
An image of his god in gold,
The which the mighty are afraid
His awful glory to behold,
Do thou, therefore, of far and near
And tongues and nations, turn your eyes
To eastward, and behold with fear
The presence ruling paradise.
Therefore,
  Princes
    Governors
     Captains
     Judges
      Treasurers
       Counselors
       Sheriffs
        And all ye rulers of the provinces,

What time you hear the flute
   Bow down;
What time you hear the harp
   Bow down;
What time the cornet
   Bow down;
What time the dulcimer
   Bow down;
What time the psaltery
   Bow down;
To the god on the Plain of Dura,
The idol of Babylon.

II

The people stood before the king
Then each man bowed before the throne;
A god is but a paltry thing,
A semblance made of gold or stone
And impotent to send or stay;
But kings cast down or elevate
According as their pleasures weigh
This way or that the scales of fate.

Therefore the congregation heard
The herald crying forth the word
Of him who reigned in Babylon.
And though each eye was cast upon
The god that looked from Dura down
They bowed in homage to the crown.
Thinking: It is our pleasure, Sir,
They bowed at the sound of the dulcimer.

Thinking: We live the King to suit,
They bowed them down at the sound of the flute.
Thinking: The King may send or stay,
The King may give or take away,
Why, then, at a little bowing carp?
They bowed them down at the sound of the harp.
With aching backs that creaked with pain
At the sound of the psaltery bowed again,
Did the princes
  The governors
    The captains
      The judges
        The treasurers
          The counselors
          The sheriffs
            And all the rulers of the provinces
              And the peoples of tongues and nations
Who came to the dedication
Of the god on the Plain of Dura,
In the province of Babylon.

Yet, though the multitude had bowed
Before him, still the mighty god
On Dura's plain stood cold and proud
Nor deigned so much as by a nod
To show acceptance of the suit
Chadnezzar and the people made;
Therefore the king sat black and mute;
Therefore the people stood afraid.

III

While divers nations bowed before
The god that stood on Dura's plain
The Hebrew children mopped the floor
Of the banquet hall with might and main.
Soon should the royal feast be spread
And lest the king a cause should find
For wrath, and lop a Hebrew head
Shadrach
  Meshach
   Abednego
Cleaned each cranny and mopped and shined
The floors, the walls and the vessels O.

No one summoned the Hebrews forth;
Why should a god require of slaves
Awe or obeisance nothing worth?
Let the cooper see to his staves
And prince and captain and counselor
Bow to the god that he be not wroth,
For he is a stench in his nostrils, Sir,
Lacking a coat of the proper cloth.
So while the nations bent their backs
Before the god on Dura's plain
Shadrach
  Meshach
   Abednego
Cleaned the crannies and scoured the cracks
And mopped the table tops once again.

The Hebrew children wiped the sweat
From burning brows and bent again
To mop and duster and pail, and yet

The sound that shivered on Dura's plain
Rattled the stones about the court
And the voices of the milling crowd
Through the windows made blurred report;
Dust from its seething came in a cloud
To plague the three in the banquet hall.
And Shadrach said:

                            Abednego
Surely the whole world comes to call;
Why are they gathered, do you know?
"Paying Chadnezzar some silly suit,
Probably praying his arms to shield
Themselves from danger, or asking loot
Their arms have won him upon the field."
Silence. The sweepers swept the dust
Once again from the thrice-swept floor
And mopped and polished, because they must,
Sill and lintel and beam and door.
Suddenly horns began to blow
And instruments of divers tones.
Listening, said Abednego:
Do you feel like bowing in your bones,
Shadrach?
 Meshach?

IV

And Shadrach answered him and said:
I hear the flute, Abednego,
Call, as the bride to the bridal bed—
Persuasive suit, Abednego,
My back is stone. I hear the harp
Twanging aloud, Abednego,
Its sound is like a summons sharp—

[39]

The kings have bowed, Abednego,
My thews are stone. The brass cornet
Cries on the air, Abednego,
To all the host at Dura met—
Princes bow there, Abednego,
My knee is stone. The dulcimer
In dulcet tone, Abednego,
Deceives my tendons, and they stir,
My will is stone, Abednego.
And now I hear the psaltery
Sound high and sweet, Abednego,
And were the heathen idol He—
Israel's God, the one true God—
I'd kiss His feet, Abednego.
But I'll not bow to idols down,
No, I'll not bow, Abednego,
For fear of black Chadnezzar's frown
To heathen gods, Abednego.
Amen.

      And Meshach cried:
The dark Chaldeans stand and stare
Looking as if they treason spied,
But I'll not bow me down, I swear,
To any but our God of old
That withered mighty Pharaoh's hand
And wrestled Israel from his hold
And led her to the promised land
Unscathed through the divided sea,
Unfamished through the wilderness.
The God of Moses, it is He—
Powerful to banish or to bless—
That worthy of all worship is.
I'll bow before no lesser god
Than our great God, the one true God,

The master of all mysteries,
The God of Israel from of old.
Amen, Amen.

To sticks and stones have men bowed down,
But I'll not bow, said Abednego;
To dead men buried underground,
To idols and images of gold
Have men bowed down in days of old.
(But I'll not bow, said Abednego.)

They peeled a stick and called it God,
Bow down, bow down, bow down, bow down;
They kneaded an image from a clod
And called it God, *bow down, bow down;*
A calf of gold did Aaron make
And in the wilderness bowed down
And offered for its brazen sake
Burnt offerings, *bow down, bow down.*
But I'll not bow in Babylon,
I'll not bow down, said Abednego,
To the gold god shining in the sun.
I'd not bow down to sticks and stones,
I'll not bow down, said Abednego;
I'd not bow down to a dead man's bones,
I'll not bow down, said Abednego.
No, I'll not bow to a god of gold,
I'll not bow down, said Abednego.
I'll bow to none but our God of old,
To Israel's God, the one true God
Will I bow down, said Abednego.
Amen, Amen, Amen, Amen.

V

Then the Chaldeans came to Chadnezzar
And whispered into his ear:
There are three Jews in Babylon
Have been here many a year.
There are three Jews in Babylon
The King lets wander free,
And these three Jews are brazen
In treason unto thee.
We have spied on them through the windows,
We have watched them through the doors
As they righted the hall for the banquet.
The sweat ran out of their pores,
They labored like honest workmen
Who had no mind to shirk
Aught at all of duty—
These hide not their hands from work,
But they are spear-spined fellows
Who never learned when to bow;
And the three Jews under Daniel
Make no obeisance now
Though the harp and flute and cornet
Sound loud and clarion-clear,
And the dulcimer declaimeth
To every listening ear
The King's decree demanding
That every nation and tongue
Bow to the God of Dura
At the sound of music and song.

Now live, O King, forever,
And if we have served thee well
Remember us with favors,
But fashion a Hebrew hell
For these three Hebrew sinners;
A furnace make seven times hot
For the sole three traitors in Babylon,
The Jews that regard thee not!

VI

Chadnezzar summoned the three and said:
Now I have heard a terrible thing,
Shadrach
  Meshach
    Abednego,
Ye bend not the knee nor bow the head
To the God of Dura, worshiping.

True, said Shadrach,
  True, said Meshach,
    True, said Abednego,
                        True, O King,
We neither kneel to the rising sun
Nor the golden god in Babylon.

Now if you bow when the flute is heard,
Now if you bow when the dulcimer
Declaims abroad my royal word
Concerning this, be as you were,

Shadrach
  Meshach
    Abednego.
But if not, then give heed to me
And learn what I design for thee.

Say on, said Shadrach.
  Say on, said Meshach.
    Say on, said Abednego.
                              Speak and say
What ill awaits us three this day;
We will neither kneel to the rising sun
Nor the golden god in Babylon.
Neither to Ra nor the god of gold,
To none but God,
                    The one true God,
The God of Israel from of old.

Chadnezzar rose in wrath and said:
There is a furnace that burns with fire
Near to hand, and by my head,
I have gotten the strange desire
To fry the fat of a traitor Jew.
And once I issue that same command,
Shadrach
  Meshach
    Abednego
Read me a riddle, and tell me *who*
Is that god shall deliver thee out of my hand?
God.
  Our God.
    The one true God.

The God of Israel from of old.
And yet if not then we will burn.
To heathen gods we may not turn.
We will neither bow to the rising sun
Nor the golden god in Babylon.
We will bow to neither nor none
But God
      Our God
             The one true God,
The God of Israel from of old.

Chadnezzar laughed into his beard
And called to a captain standing by:
As thou hast witnessed, as thou hast heard
Here are three Jews that long to fry;
See they be not deterred from it.
Summon thy mightiest men and take
Shadrach,
  And Meshach,
    And Abednego,
And cast them into the fiery pit,
But stand thou well back, for safety's sake!

VII

And they cast in Shadrach with his hat on,
  And they cast in Meshach with his shoes on,
    And they cast in Abednego with his hose on;
    They cast in the three with their clothes on,
  To perish in the fiery furnace,
Who bowed not in Babylon.

VIII

Chadnezzar stood at the furnace gate;
Seven times hot were the fiery flames.
His eyes were hard with haughty hate
And on his tongue were three cursed names:
Shadrach
  Meshach
    Abednego.

Chadnezzar stood to see their death;
His eyes were livid with cruel desire.
But suddenly the king sucked in his breath
For a fourth man walked amidst the fire
With Shadrach
  Meshach
    And Abednego.

Chadnezzar spoke to his counselors:
Were not the Hebrew children three
That we cast into the furnace, Sirs?
Aye, said they.
        Well, look, said he,
And tell me now, or burn the same,
Who is the fourth man in the flame
With Shadrach
  Meshach
    And Abednego.

Had I seen the kingdoms of the East
Draw like a cloud about my walls
It had not shaken me in the least;
A kingdom rises, a kingdom falls

As strength is joined to a king's desire.
But who is the fourth man in the fire
With Shadrach
  Meshach
    And Abednego?

Had the locusts come up like a wind
From Egypt land to strip the fields
I had hurried the harvest to its end
And stored in stone the barley yields
And fed the swine on locust meat.
But four men with unfettered feet
Walk in the midst of the flames, and we
Cast, bound, into the fire but three:
Shadrach,
  And Meshach,
    And Abednego!

Had pestilence roared like a blast
Of foul wind from the caves of death
I had buried the dead, until the last
Man left alive gave up his breath
And bowed my head to none. *But Who*
Walks in the fire with crystal shoe?
His face is a marvel to look upon,
His eyes would beggar the rising sun.
Would he but step without the flame
I'd reverence him with a godly name;
To do him honor would I command
My scepter given into his hand.
For three in the fiery furnace wert
And there are four who have no hurt.

[47]

Three in the furnace walk to and fro,
Shadrach,
  And Meshach,
    And Abednego,
And a fourth in raiment of crystal spun
Who hath a face like God's own Son.
(And never a face like the god of gold.)

IX

Chadnezzar then to the pit came near
And into the fiery furnace spoke:
Shadrach,
  Meshach,
    Abednego,
Ye in the midst of the furnace whither
I cast ye down, I pray come hither.
    The three came stumbling from the smoke
And the king began to shake in fear
As they came forth—and were but three.
    The fourth, the king said, where is he?
Ah, said Shadrach,
  Ah, said Meshach,
    Ah, said Abednego,
Look and see!
That one that came and saved us all
Is fired in the brick of the furnace wall.
That is his eye you call the sun;
That is his sound where waters run;
That is his color that reds the blood;
That is his fluid that flows in flood;
That is him bowing where forests bend;
That is his breathing you call the wind;

His is the fury that flames in fire;
Storm and trouble are of his ire;
Mercy and justice are of his mind;
His is the presence in space divined;
The hurt and the sorrowful understand
That hope and healing are of his hand;
Time is his patience abstained from wrath;
Space is his garden and light his path;
He is the shining secure from blot,
Rose, and remembrance of things forgot;
He is span of space and the sparrow's flight,
Carls and kingdoms are in his sight
Who is immortal and infinite,
Zion and Eden past Adam's fall,
First and forever and only and all!
   We that in the furnace wert
Came forth free and have no hurt
Because we harbored in the hold
Of God,
        Our God,
                The one true God,
The God of Israel from of old!

x

Chadnezzar, King of Babylon,
Turned from the three the fire had tried
To his gold god shining in the sun,
And he saw it was the shape of his pride.
And as his pride began to fade
The monstrous god that he had made
Settled slowly into the plain
Like melting ice, and left no stain.

Disdain went from its countenance
And then its jewelled eyes, all at once,
As pride washed from Chadnezzar's mind,
Lost luster like a man's struck blind.
The threescore cubits of its height
Shrank soon to two, and soon the light
From golden gilding failed to flash.
The gold god turned the color of ash
And a wind that from that quarter stirred
Spoke in sighs the people heard
And blew across the crowd to bear
Ashes to dust Chadnezzar's hair.

  When looking out to Dura's plain
He saw the golden god was gone
Never to blazon his pride again,
Chadnezzar mounted his golden throne
And lifted up his voice and cried:
(And the people heard him and replied:)

There is a God no man has seen
(Blessed be the God of Shadrach)
Whose angel this day in the pit has been
(Blessed be the God of Meshach)
To guard those who have trusted Him,
(Blessed be the God of Abednego)
And, behold, He hath delivered them!
BLESSED BE THE GOD THE HEBREWS KNOW!

What god is like unto this great God?
(Only the God of Shadrach)
Who hath bent the king's word like a rod
(Only the God of Meshach)
To give of Himself a good report!
(Only the God of Abednego)

What god can deliver after this sort?
ONLY THE GOD THE HEBREWS KNOW!

What is the will of the people then?
(Only what is the King's will)
How shall we deal with these three men?
(The King is king in Babylon still)
Then the three that out of the furnace won
Shadrach
  And Meshach
    And Abednego
Shall be promoted in Babylon!
(The King hath spoken it, it is so!)
Then the peoples of tongues and nation,
The princes
  The governors
    The captains
      The judges
        The treasurers
          The counselors
          The sheriffs
            And all the rulers of the provinces
Returned to their own stations
From the great court of Chadnezzar
In the province of Babylon.

So is all the story told
  And blessed be God
    The one true God
      The God of Israel from of old.
Amen, Amen, Amen, Amen, Amen, Amen, Amen.

THE POOR MAN'S LAMB

II SAMUEL, 12

Nathan cried out at David's door:
There were two men in one city
And one was rich and the other was poor,
A poor and a rich man, David.

Listen, O David, unto my words,
The rich man who lived in the city
Had exceeding many flocks and herds,
Many flocks had the rich man, David.

The poor man had but one little ewe,
One little ewe lamb, O David,
It might have been a daughter, he loved it so,
The poor man's ewe lamb, David.

There came a traveler to the town
Of the poor and the rich man, David.
At fall of eve he was bedded down
At the house of the rich man, David.

But the rich would spare for the wayfarer
No meat for to feed him, David,
And the poor man's lamb, he has stolen her
To dress for the traveler, David.

A moment's silence enclosed the two,
Enclosed the king and the prophet;
And the poor man's lamb, his one little ewe
Stood between Nathan and David.

Then from the hall rang David's cry:
Who was this rich man, Nathan?
For by my hand he shall surely die,
Shall surely die, cried David.

(Now he has spoken the living truth
As ever I breathe, thought Nathan,
He shall be slayer and slain, forsooth,
But I would be neither, thought Nathan.

His word could scatter my flesh as dust
To the wailing winds, thought Nathan;
Yet though I die I must do what I must,
For the flesh is cheap, thought Nathan.)

Nathan stood with his staff in his hand,
At David's door stood Nathan,
And he cried to the King: Thou art the man.
Thou art the man, O David!

For thou hast taken the Hittite's wife,
The poor man's ewe lamb, David;
And twined him of life in the battle's strife,
In the forefront of battle, David.

And God shall deal with the King, alas,
As the King with the Hittite, David.
The sword from thy house shall never pass
Because thou hast sinned so, David.

I will raise up evil within his house,
Even God has decreed it, David.
To strangers I'll give his wives to spouse.
The Lord hath spoken it, David.

I shall bring the things in secret done,
God bade me say to thee, David,
To the sight of Israel and the sun.
So God will do, even, David.

A pall was over David's sight
As he stood in the presence of Nathan,
And he saw Bathsheba in the night
As he harkened to the voice of Nathan.

The seed that is planted in the dark,
In the opened furrow, David,
Comes up at length for the sun to mark,
Be it barley or bane, O David.

And even so from the woman's womb
Will the seed emerge, O David;
In the fields of flesh thou hast sown thy doom;
Thou hast sinned against God, O David.

For God hath judged thee, and never I,
I had dealt with thee differently, David,
Not thou, but the son of thy sin shall die—
I had favored the innocent, David!

And Nathan departed from David's door;
I have done what I must, thought Nathan.
But David stood still and his heart was sore,
And prophecy came to David.

He looked to the years that were still ahead
And saw two shapes through the cloudy air:
A young girl ravished upon her bed,
And a young man hanging by his hair.
"My God, O my God!" cried David.

THE WEAVER

When I was a lass as I wove with a will
(The sound of the shuttle is a sighing sound)
My foot on the treadle it never grew still.
(Sing treadle-trid-treadle the wheel it goes round)

Was it counterpane or a tablecloth
(The sound of the shuttle is a sighing sound)
The household wanted? I wove them both.
(Sing treadle-trid-treadle the wheel it goes round)

Or carpet or clothing for backs grown bare?
(The sound of the shuttle is a sighing sound)
I wove them all with a merry, merry air.
(Sing treadle-trid-treadle the wheel it goes round)

Then in came a stranger and stood in the room
(The sound of the shuttle is a sighing sound)
Saying, "What sort of cloth do you weave in your loom?"
(Sing treadle-trid-treadle the wheel it goes round)

"Jeans for my father I weave," I said.
(The sound of the shuttle is a sighing sound)
"What would you weave if your father were dead?"
(Sing treadle-trid-treadle the wheel it goes round)

I answered him bold through the whirring loud,
(The sound of the shuttle is a sighing sound)
"If my father were dead I would weave him a shroud."
(Sing treadle-trid-treadle the wheel it goes round)

"Weave," said the stranger and vanished away.
 (The sound of the shuttle is a sighing sound)
 A shroud for my father I wove that day.
 (Sing treadle-trid-treadle the wheel it goes round)

There is a weaver whose thread is the years
 (The sound of the shuttle is a sighing sound)
 Who weaves us a mantle of joys and fears.
 (Sing treadle-trid-treadle the wheel it goes round)

As I was a-weaving as Carlton's wife
 (The sound of the shuttle is a sighing sound)
 In came the stranger as stern as strife.
 (Sing treadle-trid-treadle the wheel it goes round)

"The cloth you are weaving is bride's-bed blue."
 (The sound of the shuttle is a sighing sound)
 "I am weaving a cloth to cover us two."
 (Sing treadle-trid-treadle the wheel it goes round)

"But what if you slept alone to-night?"
 (The sound of the shuttle is a sighing sound)
 "I'd weave me a cover as black as blight."
 (Sing treadle-trid-treadle the wheel it goes round)

"Weave," said the stranger and vanished away.
 (The sound of the shuttle is a sighing sound)
 A widow's habit I wove that day.
 (Sing treadle-trid-treadle the wheel it goes round)

Time is the weaver of curious cloth
 (The sound of the shuttle is a sighing sound)
 Threaded with sorrow and joy both.
 (Sing treadle-trid-treadle the wheel it goes round)

As I was a-weaving to suit my son
(The sound of the shuttle is a sighing sound)
The stranger appeared as he first had done.
(Sing treadle-trid-treadle the wheel it goes round)

"What are you weaving?" he asked aloud.
(The sound of the shuttle is a sighing sound)
"Cloth," I countered, "to swaddle or shroud;
(Sing treadle-trid-treadle the wheel it goes round)

"Soft was the fleece and white is the thread . . ."
(The sound of the shuttle is a sighing sound)
"Shroud," said the stranger, "your son is dead."
(Sing treadle-trid-treadle the wheel it goes round)

In the web of time the warp is light
(The sound of the shuttle is a sighing sound)
But the weft is thrid with the threads of night.
(Sing treadle-trid-treadle the wheel it goes round)

The thread through my fingers grew slack and slow,
(The sound of the shuttle is a sighing sound)
And in came the stranger and saw it so.
(Sing treadle-trid-treadle the wheel it goes round)

"You have woven the sheets for your bridal bed,
(The sound of the shuttle is a sighing sound)
"You have woven your husband's shroud," he said.
(Sing treadle-trid-treadle the wheel it goes round)

"You have woven the grave clothes for your son,
(The sound of the shuttle is a sighing sound)
"Yet one piece more and your weaving is done."
(Sing treadle-trid-treadle the wheel it goes round)

Now I am weaving that nameless cloak,
(The slowing shuttle has a rattling sound)
That *thrum* was the sound of the thread as it broke . . .
(Sing treadle-trid-treadle the wheel runs down
  Runs down
    Runs down
Sing treadle-trid-treadle the wheel it runs down.)

A VOYAGE OF SOME IMPORTANCE

From Southampton, England
Sept. 6, 1620

Southampton saw two ships set sail
At the tag end of the year
When winds out of the east prevail,
Northwestward for to steer.

A stout ship was the first tall ship
That set her prow to the wave;
A curst ship was the next tall ship
That did set sail so brave.

The first ship, tight as a brewery vat,
The worst the waves could give
Tossed from her bows; the other sat
In the sea like a sailing sieve.

"Turn back, turn back," the captain cried
Who governed in her hold
As that curst ship took in the tide
That carried her on so bold.

Southampton saw that ship return
Half sinking to the quay
With the stout ship tagging at her stern;
Though she chafed at the delay

She would not sail till her sister ship
Came tacking in her wake
Past Land's End where the water's lip
Is bulged with chalky cake.

Twice over did that curst ship thrust
Her bows into the sea;
Twice like a tin tub riddled with rust
Shipping the tide sailed she.

"No more, no more," her captain cried
The third time she sank down.
"Who'd man this ship in the running tide
Would board her but to drown!"

The Speedwell was that curst ship's name
But she sped not well at all.
Her crowd aboard the stout ship came
Northwestward for to haul.

Southampton saw one ship set sail,
Her wake as white as snow
And the passengers cheering at the rail,
For a fine small gale did blow.

The stout ship she was broad of beam
With castles fore and aft,
And she flew like a phantom ship in a dream
And the sea flew by her and laughed.

Her passengers stood at the rail
Or hunkered in the hold
As the stout ship flew beneath her sail
Northwest into the cold.

November frosted on the plank
Before the log was done,
And dismal days rose up and sank
Behind a doleful sun.

And storms burst on that quaking ship
While her wards prayed in their beds
As the knotty hand of the wind did rip
Her cracking sails to shreds.

And still northwest the course was set,
The wake to southeast shone,
Nor fore nor aft was landfall yet,
Though full three months were gone

Since Land's End vanished in the sea,
Her head in grey mist furled;
And round them was infinity
And water was their world

With neither north nor south nor west
Nor east, but only sky
Above and sea about, and crest
Of wave to mark them by.

Yet of the hundred souls and two
That out of Leyden came
The same did every morn renew
The voyage in God's name.

And in God's name they would prevail
Whatever brimmed their cup,
For when the sky let down in hail
Their courage it rose up.

Three months crept past and twice four days
And then the morning broke
At last on land that through the haze
Looked like a wisp of smoke.

The long boats beached soon on the sand;
And Martin's motley flock
Stepped from the sea upon the land
At a place called Plymouth Rock.

MARRY THE MOON

Word of it got to his work-bent ear
High on the hill as he cut the trees,
Low in the valley he came to clear
Word of it went like the buzz of bees.
Once he heard it he knew no rest,
Once he knew it he heard no sound
But the wild thing beating within his breast
Like the sexton's tread on graveyard ground.

Log butt, tree top, all he saw
Changed at once to a lovely face
Coveted, courted, held in awe,
Palmed and kissed at the trysting place
Hard by the waters of Clayburn Creek
Deep in the wood that has no name,
Feathery soft on either cheek,
Full on the lips that seared like flame.

Let the lintel fall to the sill,
The rooftree sag and the open sky
Look through the rafters; let the hill
Return to sedge, now green with rye
To gladden the bride that will not look
Far from the window to see it grow;
Forget the footlog to span the brook,
Forget in the spring of the year to sow.

Forget, forget; but tell her this,
O tell her this to cause her pain:
"Because your heart that was mine is his
I never shall darken your door again.

Should any missing me seek in sorrow
Send them down to the pool to seek,
For there I marry the moon tomorrow
At noon of night in Clayburn Creek."

AS I WAS WALKING THE WIDE ROAD

Three Stations

As I was walking the wide road
Without nowhere to go
The meanest wind was blowing abroad
That ever had breath to blow,
   Blow, blow,
That ever had breath to blow.

Its touch was like a saber
That cleaves the white flesh clean;
Had any man dwelt my neighbor
Its cut had been less keen,
   Keen, keen,
Its cut had been less keen.

As I was walking the dark street
Without nowhere to bide
The hardest stones were under my feet
That ever were struck with stride,
   O, O,
That ever were struck with stride.

Than marble they were colder
That paves the church dooryard;
Had any hand touched my shoulder
They had not been so hard,
   So hard,
They had not been so hard.

As I was walking without love
Along the endless road
The heart in my side was heavy enough
Alone to make a load,
   Load, load,
Alone to make a load.

It was that weight that drove me
To the hole I dropped it in;
Had any had care to love me
I had not died till then,
   Till then,
O I had not died till then.

III

SONGS FOR BREATH

THE SERVICE OF SONG

The apple the bough let fall
To ease a too bounteous store
And deemed it no matter at all
Is withered to its core.

There is nothing left to define
Its glow as it hung on the bough,
And yet the service is mine
To restore it now.

To restore it where earthward it hung
Pendant on slender stem,
For this is the service of song:
To brighten the dim

Coin of a kingdom whose king
Lies centuries asleep,
To render the humblest thing
To memory's keep.

FROM WHENCE IS SONG

Though I have drunk the waters of that spring
From whence is song, if it be God's or no
I cannot tell; nor why its currents sing
Nor by what secret ways they sometimes flow
Like desert rivers sucked into the ground
To leave the traveler who seeks their tide,
And dreams he hears far off their welcome sound,
With thirst the greater for the drink denied.

That wizard water waits upon our need
To strike it from the burning silt of drought
That we be pilgrim to its currents freed,
As to that stream that from the rock gushed out
Turned all of Israel from upbraiding God
When Moses, grown desperate, smote it with his rod.

A SONG FOR BREATH

Who found in honor scanty food
Craved communion with the dead
To learn if immortality
In art were recompense for want,
And image struck from out the eye
And the quick brain strewn all abroad.
Beside a poet's grave he stood
As midnight gathered to the stroke
Of twelve, and spoke:

Now, Poet, housed beneath the ground,
Camped in the shadow of the stone
That spells your name without a sound,
To silicates of silence gone,
Gather again to speech and tell
Me if remembrance of the songs
You shaped so sure and wildly well
They minstrels make unwilling tongues
Is comfort to you in the grave.
In summer when the booted grain
Is wimpled as an ocean wave
Or in the wind aslant like rain,
Is earth the softer where you lie,
Your flesh less slack about the bone
Because you saw in days gone by
And said in sonnets how it shone?

Or in the autumn when the wind
Is elegy, and the green grass
By autumn's harmful hand is thinned
And the thief-fingered days that pass

Strew the harsh earth with stolen loot,
Do you remember and rejoice
At how the shrunk and shriveled fruit
Is shapely still because your voice
Gave it a contour neither time
Nor frost can wizen out of shape,
The apple firm gold in a rhyme,
And clear in an image the globed grape?

Or are the nights you lay abed
Cold to the marrow of your bone
Warmed in the dust, now men have said
Your songs are durable as stone?
And are the hungers one and all
That ate like acid through your frame
And tasted on the tongue was gall
Fed by the froth of latter fame?
And is the hand you reached toward love,
Like some cold beggar's to a fire,
To meet a fist in a mailed glove
Full now with the feel of your desire?

In a blue space of silence stood
Upright the ghost from out the grave;
The mouthless face beneath the shroud
Clacked all its bones and answer gave:

When that which set the beat of song
Stilled in the sure clock at my wrist
From which the wizard hand was hung
That wrought the magic songs, from mist
Of meaning which the force of thought
Gave shapes as shimmering and proud
As crystal kingdoms clear of fault

Cast from the chaos of a cloud,
To set its signet past the rage
Of time, immortal signature
Imprinted on some fragile page
Stronger than marble to endure,
I left off care. I made my songs
Of breath, and now my breath is gone
Fame strikes its sticks on silent gongs.
Once the white marrow of my bone
Relayed the rumor that the vein
Was clogged with the debris of death
The watchful sentry of the brain
Cried warnings through the camp of breath
That fell in ultimate defeat
By eternity's dark street.

The young grain threads me with its root
Who owns no taste of food or fame,
So are my former hungers fed.
Is love dust, that my hand is full?
The risen ghost at midnight said
Shaking the dry gourd of its skull
And turning to nothing, which it was
That now was nothing but a name
And atoms greening in the grass.

Rest, said the living poet then
Chewing his honor once again.

SUCH INSTANCE

A young girl took a walk
In the cool last hour of day
Among the stones of the graveyard.
A feathery spray
Of the sedge began to talk
And she cocked her head
And stood still, listening hard.
The low sedge said:

Being not beautiful
Nor here of any use
I am all ways condemned
And fire is set to my root
When frosts have nipped me dry.
Yet by dead flesh I am stemmed
And the gray stuff of a skull
When the flames begin to shoot
Flames, flames high
And bends to the wind's stroke
And passes in smoke.

The young girl trembling stood
With one foot lifted up,
Poised there about to flee
When out of the tulip's cup
Nearly the color of blood
The words came free:
With what cold constancy
Stare upon the sky
The dead who lack all sight!
From one of twin sockets I

Have sprung, the instrument
That once marked which way went
The sun, and which came night
Feeds me. And by its side
The other gaping wide,
Forsaking its bony frame,
Sees nothing the same.

The young girl turned to flee
But her foot caught in the root
Of a stout, wide-branching tree;
The headstone at its foot
In syllables of stone
Spoke a name, her own.
There leaned, as if to read
The name, a tulip there;
Around its crimson cup
Till faggot should confirm
The limit of its term,
The wavering sedge thrust up
Fine feathery tufts in air.

AS I WENT OVER THE MEADOWS

As I went over the meadows
And over the hills of Ling
I met with many a wicked
And many a saintly thing.

And which bespoke me fairer
I have not wit to say,
The saintly thing, or the wicked
That waited beside my way.

PANDORA, WHEN WE COME TO CHOOSE

Pandora, when we come to choose
The gifts you offer, turn aside
Our questing hands from pain and bruise
And sting, all in one bundle tied.
Let not greed make the choice vain:
Pandora, hide the box of pain.

IN MATTERS OF PRIDE

When I was a lad
Less than half a man tall
And fell, I had
But a little way to fall.

But as I grew older
And taller, I found
The higher my shoulder
Thrust my head from the ground

The harder I fell.
I came to full stride
Of manhood versed well
In matters of pride,

Knowing to shun
Such folly of the proud
As blindly to run
With my head in a cloud.

For the low in spirit,
As the child that's small,
Are always near it
When to earth they fall.

TO MARKET, TO MARKET

At morning-shine and shadow-fall
I see, through chill or April air,
The maggot-mass of man repair
To traffic at the Tradesman's stall.
And those go by with haughty tread
Whose pockets clink with coin; but some
Are beggars to life's market come
With not a cent to buy them bread,
And there is terror in their tread.

HEAR ME, FATHER, IT IS I

Hear me, Father, it is I
Calling to Thee from the road,
Frightened of the lowering sky,
Weighted with a weary load.
If, my Father, Thou be not
Tell it, and I shall not fear
Howsoever ill my lot;
Angry though the sky appear
Then, it's not Thy countenance
Wroth with me and man; my pack
Shall be lightened all at once:—
Thee I bear upon my back.

IF EVIL WERE A LITTLE ROAD

If evil were a little road
That led among soft leaves astir
Where late the peach and plum had snowed
A fall of flakes through April air,
And I the only traveler;
And were I certain I would find
The sorry end I have in mind
When I had traveled all the road,
Still I would journey forth and sing
A song upon the road to hell
For joy of the journeying.

I KNOW A VALLEY GREEN WITH CORN

I know a valley green with corn
Where Nottley's waters roil and run
From the deep hills where first at morn
It takes the color of the sun

And bears it burning through the shade
Of birch and willow till its tide
Pours like a pulse, and never stayed,
Dark where the Gulf's edge reaches wide.

There, while the twilight spends its dream
Of light and shadow both, the whir
Of bats and cry of doves will seem
A very liveness of the air.

About a house the ivy's foot
Creeps slowly up to hide the eaves
And wreathe the chimney, dark with soot,
Into a colonnade of leaves.

And one will loiter in the yard
Soft shadowed by the last of day
As if she waited for a word
From lips three thousand miles away

That yearn to speak against her hair
But, dumb behind the palm of space
Tauten to trembling, while there
Darkness obliterates her face.

ON CROSSING THE DESERTS
OF THE SOUTHWEST

Coming on arid country, not the mind's
But nature's, witnessed by the slabs of slag
Molten beneath the morning sun that blinds
Travelers eastward, the insensate crag
Of iron on the desert's rim was dry
And thirsted in my throat; and on my brain
Momently as the four wheels whirled us by
Weighed the unfruitful centuries of the plain.

Greater than grandeur was the look it wore;
Its verge was vision, as if one should find
Framed in the mortal sight a magic door
Time, the immortal substance, flamed behind
Permitting us of numbered days to see
The endless burning of eternity.

MIRROR

You, Sister, long lost,
Being thirty years dead,
Are secure from time's frost
That whitens the head.

She that bore you
Would find you the same,
Could the dust restore you,
As when death came.

In her heart's mirror
I look and see
A small, pale child
Gazing at me.

You were her pleasure
At rest or play,
You were her treasure
Death filched away.

Whole I behold you
In her heart's glass,
Shut in a dream
That does not pass.

WHAT SWORD, O WHAT DEFENSE

What sword, O what defense
To hand shall that one carry
Whom pale pretensions harry?
Why, cool indifference
Is cutless keen for cleaving
Himself from him deceiving
With fickle false affection
The true heart's diligence.

There came a very prince
Known to the populace;
He had a youthful face
That aged at time's expense
Into a mask to mime
The elders of old time:
The steed on which he traveled
Paced to indifference.

Said he: As I rode hence
From that place where I mounted
All chronicles accounted
The certain imminence
Of perils for my trying,
Of deaths not mine for dying
To leaden life; I journeyed
With youth's indifference.

Plain on a plain immense
As hell's far-flung foundation
The Ogre from his station
Fumed forth with vehemence;

I spilled his bloody flagon
And I slew that fiery dragon
Whose name is named and nameless
With cold indifference.

THE FIGURES ON THE STAIR

Those figures on the stair
Hale in mid-morning air
Find at one level, love,
And at the next above

Strength, wealth, or pride of place,
While in each sunlit face
The dial of time too soon
Announces afternoon.

These same who came to choose
At dawn, toward evening lose
Again along that stair
The gifts found waiting there,

But not to gather dust.
Time takes the gifts in trust
Again for those to find
Who follow on behind

These who depart in pain
Never to know again
The mortal vista, viewed
From any altitude.

THERE NEVER WAS TIME

I wish, he said, the years would linger
And fly less fast to make me old;
My face is a mask that time's swift finger
Models, moulding wrinkle and fold
In sagging flesh youth fashioned true
To the ageless image, engraved on brass,
Of a young face Rome or Athens knew.
(There was time for youth to pass.)

Time had a long look when I was twenty;
Was there anything I had not done
And yet would do? Well, there was plenty
Of daylight left in the cycling sun.
The roughs of knowledge that wanted scaling
Loomed—there was time to be a sage;
Time and to spare to heal all ailing.
(And time enough for a man to age.)

But now the night that has no breaking
Shadows the sun gone down the west,
And my heart in its damaged cage is aching
After lost years, too brief at best.
I know a journey that yet wants going,
I know a song that is still to sing,
I know a fallow that waits the sowing—
(There never was time for everything.)

THE BARGAIN

As I was going out to spend
My speech upon that iron ear
That tells to the electric wind
What all the world may hear,

I met a slow hearse on the way.
The heir of silence rode within
Whose speech, if he had aught to say,
Was not for living men

As late his laggard flesh was borne
After its fleet ghost, fled before
As imperceptibly as morn
Whitens at a door,

To claim at God's elected tent
That entry earned by slow degree
As day by day the breath was spent
To buy eternity.

They thought it quick, who vigil kept
Beside his bed and bent, afraid,
To test his sleep when last he slept,
The bargain he had made.

But barter is as long as life
For that estate which—once the breast
Is rested of its precious strife—
Seems suddenly possessed.

NARCISSUS, BY THE BORDERED POOL

Narcissus, by the bordered pool
That glassed your image clear and cool,
Vain thoughts were yours, but I beside
Your lithe form would have vainly tried
To think as vain a thought. O Fool,
To love it there, all beauty is
As vain as we, as vain as this.

THE HEART AS PLANET

The planetary heart that moves in space,
At one with worlds that tread the starry deeps,
Acknowledging the magnet of a face
About that sun a constant orbit keeps
In ceaseless cycles, being winged to wheel
Until the essence of its star glow wan
Or the great mass of death in passing steal
It from the emanations of its sun.

Then, though its nature not an atom alter,
It shall pursue a magnified ellipse
About a greater Sun that does not falter
As did the old to shut it in eclipse,
So far in space it may not reappear
To man by reason of its lengthened year.

THE ELM AND THE MOON

A girl was thinking about her lover
Under the elm tree under the moon;
She was saying over and over
A mournful chanty, a cruel croon:
Love is given me but to grieve me,
What I have given's no more to give;
Because I have given it he will leave me,
Because he will leave me I cannot live.

The moon looked down between the elm leaves,
Shadow mottled her lovely face;
She was grieving as only a girl grieves
Who has bargained her gift of grace
For knowledge tart as the taste of aloes,
For pain as sharp as the nettle's thrust,
For the garb of her who dressed in grey goes
Soberly down to a house of dust.

The girl was gone before the dawning;
The elm and the moon remained to hear
Again the voice of girlhood moaning
In summer, in winter, in the spring of the year:
Love is given me but to grieve me,
If I surrender I suffer his throes,
If I deny him then he will leave me
In tropic country shut fast by snows.

MY LOVE IT IS TWAIN

My love it is twain,
Divided for two;
He has it half again
Whose shadow are you.
Half it is yours.
Though flawed in desire
It yet endures
God's ice, your fire.
Cold flaming to coal,
Fire cooling to ice,
It is greater than whole
And baffles me twice.

SONG

Would I had a lover
To tryst with me in shadow
When the wind blows over
The asters in the meadow.

Had I but a lover,
In the windy weather
We could hide together
In the meadow's cover.

TESTAMENT

Since praise is parcel of their right
And it were seemly of the mind
To thank the donors of delight
Whose gifts are tattle toned and hued
That none who seek may fail to find,
A testament of gratitude

I make to lovely things for thanks:
The bloodroot of the March-wet wood,
The yellow susan and the banks
Of frosty asters and the rose
Bleeding with bloom from every bud;
And every broadening brook that flows

Vocal with pleasure from its spring,
And choirs that shatter from the shell
On boughs to congregate and sing,
Song birds of every name and note,
And sound of organ and of bell
Clamoring from its iron throat;

And forms and colors, roseate, round,
Curve, plane, refracted rainbow light,
Halos and emanations bound
To elder things, the phosphor ghost
Escaping from old wood at night,
And overhead the starry host;

Yea, every lovely thing I find
Whether of earth or sea or air
Crowding the doorway of my mind,
Too numberless of name to call,
For that your cumber is not care
But beauty's own, I thank you all.

THE PEACH IN BLOOM

As I was going out to plow
When March had thawed the frozen field
I saw the peach transform her bough
Into a wand of jewels, sealed
Through winter in the strictest box
Shut and secured with secret locks.

Till air or ion, no man knows,
Released at once the hidden spring
And swift as winter when it snows
Set all the boughs to blossoming,
No power could force the fragile lid
To find the blossoms where they hid.

The peach blooms made a holiday
Of fragrance under every bough,
So I was hindered on my way
As I was going out to plow,
Enchanted by the simple sight
Of peach boughs blossomed overnight.

FRUITING

The tongue is tart to match the cherry
In latter May; then lovers jower
But not for long, their tongues grow merry
When June-reds tumble in a shower.
The crabbed scolds that fault a fellow
Who comes to pay them summer suit
In apple time grow grave and mellow
To match the sweet October fruit.

The chestnut burr is spined with needles
Outside, but in is velvet-lined;
So the girl's heart a lover wheedles
Till two are of a single mind.
She learns while nervously computing
The days till she be brought to bed
That any tree that comes to fruiting
Must first its early blossom shed.

Though what boughs think about the reaping,
After the season of their care,
Of ripened harvests from their keeping
Is never told, each year they bear
Their fruit. And Tom and Teenie wedded
Bear up their young till they are lucked
With brides and grooms; then they are bedded
Barren as boughs whose fruit is plucked.

THE BIRDS
From a Child's Memory

Beyond the fields in Elder's wood
The time that I had lost myself
Because I tried to catch an elf
That wore a sort of raddled hood,
I stopped to rest, as hid as he,
Under the leaves of a little tree.

A nest upon a bough was near
On which a brooding bird could sit
On speckled eggs there were in it
Gone half asleep and have no fear.
It was hidden there so well
To find it was a miracle.

I did not touch them where they lay,
I only looked, and then a spell
Came on the nest, and every shell
Cracked open in the swiftest way
And something at each center stirred
And every egg became a bird.

And every bird began to sing
At once the weakest sort of song;
I could not wait till they sang strong
Nor stay to watch them on the wing.
I had to hunt the raddled elf
In Elder's wood, then find myself.

THE SOUND OF RAIN

I said to myself beneath the roof
One rainy night while fast they fell
From clouds with many in store for proof:
What raindrops most resemble tell.
The answer that my fancy gave,
Since it could say the thing it chose:
I think the rain sounds like a wave
As sucking down the shore it goes.

The rain was always like the sea,
I told my fancy, try again.
And then my fancy said to me:
A lot of sticks are like the rain,
A lot of sticks cut from the brakes
Of cane that by the river crowd,
And set in rows like slender stakes
With top ends reaching to the cloud.

THE SHAGGY HILLS OF HUGHLY

The shaggy hills of Hughly
That look at Pindar Lake
Cast no cool reflection
When the water is awake.

But when the water's sleeping
And steady is the sky
Then all the hills of Hughly
Deep in the water lie.

THE BROOK

From the strict woods the small brook ran
Into a meadow where it dropped
An octave down, and spread its fan
Distant to where my sight was stopped.

That wet and earth-old element
As fluent shaped as shower and sea
In the green grammar where it went
Defined itself as simile;

Being as one-way set, as strong
In will, which always is to flow,
As loud in hindrance turned to song
As that old, ageless stream I know

That courses closer to the bone
From its wild fount which is the heart
Than water washes the drowned stone
In pale and perfect counterpart.

THE HERD

From Langdon Ridge the cattle stare
On wide blue meadows of the air.
They crop about the boulder's foot
Spare grass to stave away their want

And staff them with a cud to chew
Through twilights when the fall of dew
Makes little showers from shaken boughs
Under the oak trees where they house;

Or in the noonday's utter blaze
When splotched with shade they like to laze
As still, except when blue-flies pass,
As horned Buddhas in the grass.

In aimless echelons they crop
The scant fare of the mountain top,
Careless until the frost has come
And boys are sent to herd them home

To scanter mangers in the shed
Than nature's, out of which they fed
With patient and intrepid tongue
In niggard woods all summer long.

THE MARINERS

The fleets of leaves that summered at their docks
In drowsy harbors have uplifted sail
And stagger in passage, as their prows prevail
To airy oceans, through wind-lifted locks.
With tattered canvas and unlighted prows
Darkly deport the fragile mariners
Upon whatever course the wind that stirs
Their sails to motion bears them from the boughs.

The sailing earth that lists not to his tread
Bears man the mariner of space, and he
A moment now may turn away his head,
Or drowse and waken by a cold country
To find his decks converted in a trice
To iron in the artifice of ice.

COUNTRY AUTUMN

This is that season when the sun
Is furtive on its journey south;
And autumn's viney vessels run
Rare wine that reds the fox's mouth
And marks the bland opossum's sign
Dribbled under the wild grapevine.

Spring is a miser with her goods,
Granting at most the tasty cherry
To hungry lips; the summer woods
Are prodigal with the blackberry
Heavy in thorny branches hung,
And the blueberry to tempt the tongue.

But autumn is the rich provider:
Now bin and cellar are stored with fruit
Of several sort, and apple cider
Gushes to pails at the press' foot;
The erstwhile round and purple grape
Liquid has learned a vessel's shape.

The squirrel that's swift abroad has put
Aside while shortening days depart
The walnut and the hickory nut
And acorn in the oak tree's heart
To stead him when the wind is loud
And snow flies from a frozen cloud.

The rabbit lines his builded burrow
With velvet furze to keep him warm
And ground mice tread their hollow furrow
On errands augurous of storm,

While loud the wild grouse sounds his drum
Afield, announcing winter come.

Not snow's approach nor autumn's waning
Startles their battened domiciles;
The deepening flood of red leaves raining
In crackling currents down the hills
Bears to their caves no bruit of death
To shake their safe or cozened breath.

And I that glean the glutted season
Of fruit against the hour of need
Fear not the rack of want, nor treason
In that germane within the seed
The while my hand be not denied
Strength and scope to sow them wide.

A CERTAIN ESSENCE OF THE SUN

A certain essence of the sun,
Its autumn aspect in the trees,
Suddenly shot my sight beyond
What simple vision sees,

And I was looking at despair.
It had no shape, it kept no form,
It was like judgment altered air
Renders of coming storm.

Yet doubtless; and I stared it through
And saw the mountains west of night
Founded in a changeless view
In my perishing sight

That from their granite stay,
Like shot against a stone,
On terror's tangent flashed away
Into the dark unknown.

WINTRY SHADOW

Hardly six months away from June,
The bright and temperate afternoon
Was mild as spring's or summer's, still
The air contained a certain chill

No instrument might register
But witnessed by the constant chirr
Of crickets hid in leafy gold
Complaining shrilly of a cold

My calendar had not embraced
Until that moment when I faced
Skyward, and saw the waning sun
Shine ghostly through a skeleton,

And one leaf shaking on a bough
Whose spectral substance cast, somehow,
As late November light declined,
Its wintry shadow on my mind.

MANKIN'S SONG

Under the elm tree, under the cherry,
Under the oak tree in the glen,
I have been miserable and merry,
And merry and miserable again.

Beneath the rooftree, beneath the rafter,
Beneath the wide arch of the years
My tears have all rippled into laughter,
My laughter has taggled into tears.

I have given one coin to pay the piper,
I have piped one tune for the selfsame fee;
The corn I carried to the hopper
Returned again as meal to me.

And even-steven's a bargain surely;
Each was given my good regard
If winter was hard when spring was early
And spring was early when winter hard.

WHEN I THINK OF CHRISTMAS TIME

When I think of Christmas time
It's not of candlestick nor chime,
It's not of bells nor mistletoe;
It's of a Babe born long ago.

And when about a child I think
It's not of heir to princely rank
All richly wrapped and rocked with awe,
But it's of Christ whose crib was straw.

And when to Christ I turn my mind
I do not think how He was kind;
I think of sore wounds in His side,
I think how on the cross He died.

And when I think about His death
The very thought alarms my breath,
Not that He died the death of men,
But that I slew Him with my sin.

And when I think that it was I
Who raised the cross on Calvary
My tears like salty rivers run
For Christ my Lord who hanged thereon.

And when my Lord beholds my tears
He speaks to quiet me of my fears:
How is it thou hast slain Me, say,
Who am but born this Christmas day?

Who am but born at morning-shine
In thy own heart's Palestine—
Born to suffer and be tried
Before the Pilate of thy pride—

Born to sweat in agony
In thy soul's Gethsemane—
Born, between a loun and thief,
To hang upon thy unbelief?

Thou unto My tomb shall come
In thy faith's Jerusalem
And behold it bare, and find
Easter breaking in thy mind.

Therefore let My Birthday be
A time of joyful jubilee.
With the Host hosannas sing;
I am born anew to be thy King
On Christmas day,
On Christmas day,
On Christmas day in the morning.

SINCE CHRIST WAS A LAMB O

Since Christ was a lamb O
    A lamb O,
    A lamb O,
Since Christ was a lamb O
Blessed are the sheep.
When they are far from fold O
    From fold O,
    From fold O,
When they are far from fold O
He guards them from the steep.

Since Christ was a child O
    A child O,
    A child O,
Since Christ was a child O
Blessed children are.
Because they are mild O
    Are mild O,
    Are mild O,
Because they are mild O
He guides them from afar.

Since Christ was a man O
    A man O,
    A man O,
Since Christ was a man O
Then blessed are men.
But meriting His mercy O
    His mercy O,
    His mercy O,
But meriting His mercy O
Because they turn from sin.

Since Christ came to save O,,
    To save O,
    To save O,
Since Christ came to save O
Blessed are we all;
The lamb in the fold O,
    The fold O,
    The fold O,
The child in His hold O
And men who heed His call.

THE COMFORTERS

When I was sore afflicted
And lay for long abed
My comforters evicted
The senses from my head

With ache and symptom numbered
On fingertip and thumb
Till forty were encumbered
And death loomed in the sum.

And, dressed in cleric's robe,
Bildad harassed the sinner,
As once he harried Job
All day without his dinner.

JEHOVAH BLEW MY SHARDS TO FORM

Jehovah blew my shards to form
From chaos; I arose
The shape of man. What next the norm
He means for me none knows,

As through my cells His prophets go,
Crying along the vein:
Jehovah takes His breath to blow
On chaos come again.

GRAMMAR OF BEING

My head with all its hurtful hive
Of thoughts has failed to fathom quite
Past, present, future of alive,
And yet I parse it day and night.

My heart accepts its living flood
Unmindful if it fail but once
To issue its edict of blood
Then life would wither in its fonts.

My breathing breast has yet to win
The word for life I wait to shout,
Yet momently I draw life in
And momently I breathe it out.

O ELEMENTS

I who must bear the ceaseless rage
Of constant war with time, engage
Always the foe, therefore to see
The sun at morn is victory.

Seeking alliances, I plead
With all things succoring my need,
And count it nothing less than right
The elements by my side should fight.

O Sun, when time has conquered me
Diminished shall your rising be,
Or if my death by day be met
Direly depleted shall you set.

Consider, Air, when I shall keep
A silence death-ordained and deep,
By so much less shall be your note
As shakes the lyre-box of my throat.

O wayward Water, running down
With vocal flow by field and town,
Remember, when with death I go
Lessened shall all your currents flow.

Now, therefore, be for armament
And moat repelling death's advent,
O Air and Water. Be, O Sun,
The signal yet of victory won.

And Earth, my sister element,
The two of us were never meant,
Incestuous, or without delight
To lie together in the night:

Therefore if death should plead for me
A lover's suit, reject his plea.
Though he compel me to his will
Reject me still, reject me still!

THREE EPIGRAPHS

I: FOR BOW DOWN IN JERICHO

From chips and shards, in idle times,
I made these stories, shaped these rhymes;
May they engage some friendly tongue
When I am past the reach of song.

II: FOR BETTER A DINNER OF HERBS

I was of greater stature than
At finish, when this work began.
Each reader as he sloughs the gloss
To read beneath will meet my loss;
And may he out of charity
Add my cubits back to me.

III: FOR BALLAD OF THE BONES

Being a pedagogue confined
Within four walls, to ease my mind
Far from Dooly's dales and stones
I visited the Place of Bones,
And as they knit to life I saw
And of that wonder wrote with awe.

When I have learned what death may teach
And my bones, stricken each from each,
Lie in some hole or hollow dim
May some Ezekiel speak to them
And they rise up from ruin rife,
Leaping to everlasting life.

Printed in the United States
51344LVS00001B/259-279